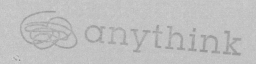anythink

D0803289

True or False?

Weather

Daniel Nunn

Raintree

Chicago, Illinois

Edited by Dan Nunn, Rebecca Rissman,
and Catherine Veitch
Designed by Joanna Hinton-Malivoire
Picture research by Ruth Blair
Production by Victoria Fitzgerald
Originated by Capstone Global Library
Printed and bound in China by Leo Paper Products
Limited

17 16 15 14 13 12
10 9 8 7 6 5 4 3 2 1

Library of Congress Cataloging-in-Publication Data
Nunn, Daniel.
True or False? Weather / Daniel Nunn.
p. cm.—(True or false?)
Includes bibliographical references and index.
ISBN 978-1-4109-5070-3 (hb)—ISBN 978-1-4109-5076-5
(pb) 1. Weather—Juvenile literature. I. Title.
QC981.3.N86 2013
551.6—dc23   2012019715

Acknowledgments
We would like to thank the following for permission
to reproduce photographs: iStockphoto pp. 4
(© Grady Reese), 13 (© luoman), 20 (© Judy
Barranco); Shutterstock pp. 4 (© Smit, © Algecireño, ©
BestPhotoByMonikaGniot), 5 (© Iakov Kalinin, © Alinute
Silzeviciute), 6 (© grafvision), 7 (© AISPIX by Image
Source, © topora), 8 and back cover (© Valua Vitaly),
9 (© Bas Meelker), 10 (© Anest), 11 and back cover (©
Loskutnikov, © cardiae), 12 (© Lars Christensen), 13 (©
UgputuLf SS), 14 (© Nazzu), 15 (© Christopher Elwell, ©
cobalt88), 16 (© WDG Photo), 17 (© Poznyakov), 18 (©
Pigprox), 19 (© FWStupidio), 21 (© Pincasso), 22 (© Jhaz
Photography).

Cover photographs reproduced with permission of
Shutterstock (© Iakov Kalinin (palm tree scene), ©
Gorilla (snowman)).

Every effort has been made to contact copyright holders
of any material reproduced in this book. Any omissions
will be rectified in subsequent printings if notice is given
to the publisher.

Contents

The Weather

There are lots of different types of weather. How much do **YOU** know about the weather?

What to Wear

We wear coats, hats, and scarves when the weather is hot and sunny.

✔ **True or false?** ✘

✖ False!

We wear coats, hats, and scarves
when the weather is cold. The clothes
keep us warm!

Sunglasses

We wear sunglasses
when the weather is
cloudy and gloomy.

✔ **True or false?** ✘

✕ False!

We wear sunglasses when the weather is sunny. The sunglasses help protect our eyes from the bright sun.

Snow

Snow is made of frozen water.

✔ True!

Snow is made of frozen water.
Frozen water is called ice.

Clouds

Clouds are made of cotton wool.

 True or false?

11

✖ False!

Clouds are not made of cotton wool.
Clouds are made of lots of teeny, tiny
drops of water.

Fog

Fog is made of clouds that are near the ground.

✔ **True!**

Fog is made of clouds that are near the ground. It can be difficult to see very far on a foggy day.

Wind

Wind can make your television work!

✔ True!

Wind turbines like these use wind to make electricity. Electricity makes televisions and other gadgets work.

Weather for Kites

People fly kites when
the weather is windy.

 True or false?

✔ True!

People fly kites when the weather is windy. If there is no wind, the kites do not fly.

Umbrellas

People use umbrellas to go flying on a windy day.

 True or false?

19

✖ False!

People do not use umbrellas to fly. People put up umbrellas on a rainy day to keep dry.

Thunder

We hear thunder when an airplane flies into a cloud.

✔ **True or false?** ✗

✖ False!

Thunder is not made when an airplane flies into a cloud. Thunder is the noise made by lightning!

Can You Remember?

What keeps us warm when the weather is cold?
What keeps us dry on a rainy day?
What protects our eyes from the bright sun?

Look back through the book to check your answers.

Index

Activity

Make Your Own True or False Game

Help your child make a Weather: True or False game. Collect a selection of pictures of the weather from magazines. Mount each picture on cardboard. Then with the child, write a series of true or false statements about the weather in the pictures on separate pieces of cardboard. Put one statement with each corresponding picture. On the back of each picture, write if the statement is true or false. For the game, read the statement out loud, ask the child if it is true or false, then have the child turn over the picture to check if he or she is correct. To extend the activity, ask the child to write the statements and whether they are true or false, and then ask you the questions.